Contents

Some words are shown in bold, **like this**.
You can find out what they mean by looking in the glossary.

Introduction

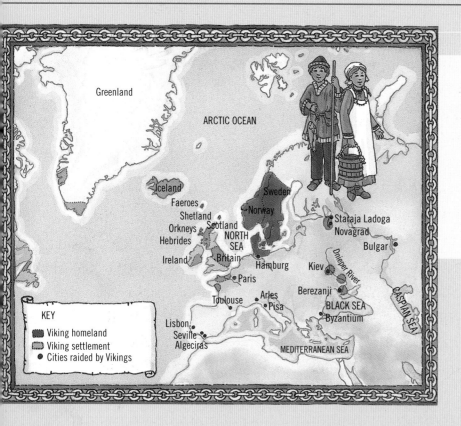

Greenland

ARCTIC OCEAN

Iceland
Faeroes
Shetland
Orkneys Scotland
Hebrides NORTH
SEA
Ireland Britain
Paris
Toulouse Arles
Pisa
Lisbon
Seville
Algeciras MEDITERRANEAN SEA

Sweden
Norway
Staraja Ladoga
Novagrad
Bulgar
Hamburg Kiev Dnieper River
Berezanji
BLACK SEA
Byzantium
CASPIAN SEA

KEY
■ Viking homeland
▨ Viking settlement
● Cities raided by Vikings

This map shows
how far the
Vikings travelled
to raid and settle.

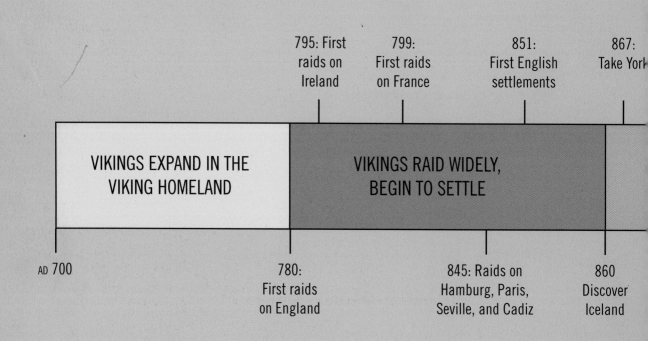

795: First
raids on
Ireland

799:
First raids
on France

851:
First English
settlements

867:
Take York

VIKINGS EXPAND IN THE
VIKING HOMELAND

VIKINGS RAID WIDELY,
BEGIN TO SETTLE

AD 700

780:
First raids
on England

845: Raids on
Hamburg, Paris,
Seville, and Cadiz

860
Discover
Iceland

The VIKINGS

Revised and Updated

JANE SHUTER

Heinemann
LIBRARY

www.heinemann.co.uk/library
Visit our website to find out more information about Heinemann Library books.

To order:
 Phone 44 (0) 1865 888066
 Send a fax to 44 (0) 1865 314091
 Visit the Heinemann Bookshop at www.heinemann.co.uk/library to browse our catalogue and order online.

First published in Great Britain by Heinemann Library, Halley Court, Jordan Hill, Oxford OX2 8EJ, part of Harcourt Education.
Heinemann is a registered trademark of Harcourt Education Ltd.

© Harcourt Education Ltd 1998, 2007
Second edition first published in paperback in 2008
The moral right of the proprietor has been asserted.

Editorial: Clare Lewis
Design: Richard Parker and Q2A Solutions
Picture Research: Hannah Taylor and Ruth Blair
Production: Helen McCreath

Printed and bound at WKT Ltd

13 digit ISBN 978 0 431 07685 0 (hardback)
11 10 09 08 07
10 9 8 7 6 5 4 3 2 1

13 digit ISBN 978 0 431 07742 0 (paperback)
12 11 10 09 08
10 9 8 7 6 5 4 3 2 1

British Library Cataloguing in Publication Data
Shuter, Jane
History Opens Windows: The Vikings
948'.022
A full catalogue record for this book is available from the British Library.

Acknowledgements
The publishers would like to thank the following for permission to reproduce photographs:
pp. **6, 8, 9, 13, 20, 22, 23, 26, 29** C. M. Dixon; pp. **10, 17** Werner Forman Archive, Statens Historiska Museum, Stockholm; p. **11** Werner Forman Archive; p. **12** Werner Forman Archive, Viking Ship Museum, Bygdoy; p. **15** Courtesy of Maine State Museum, Augusta, ME; p. **16** Statens Historiska Museum; p. **24** National Museum of Ireland; p. **25** York Archeological Trust; p. **28** Macduff Everton/Corbis; p. **30** Erich Lessing, Art Resource, NY.

Illustrations: pp. **4, 14** Eileen Mueller Neill; pp. **7** Juvenal "Marty" Martinez; pp. **19, 21, 27** John James

Cover photograph reproduced with permission of The Art Archive / Oldsammlung Oslo / Dagli Orti.

Every effort has been made to contact copyright holders of any material reproduced in this book. Any omissions will be rectified in subsequent printings if notice is given to the publishers.

The Vikings lived in Norway, Denmark, and Sweden about 1,200 years ago. Starting in about AD 780, the Vikings **raided**, traded, and settled in more and more places in Europe, Iceland, Greenland, and North America. In their language, *viking* meant both "to travel" and "a pirate raid".

The Vikings were not a single group ruled by one king. Different groups of Vikings raided and traded in different places. But to the rest of the world, they were all Vikings. They spoke the same language, worshipped the same gods, and followed the same pattern of raiding and trading with countries before settling there. By about AD 1000 these groups had stopped "viking". They settled down and married local people. They were not Vikings any more.

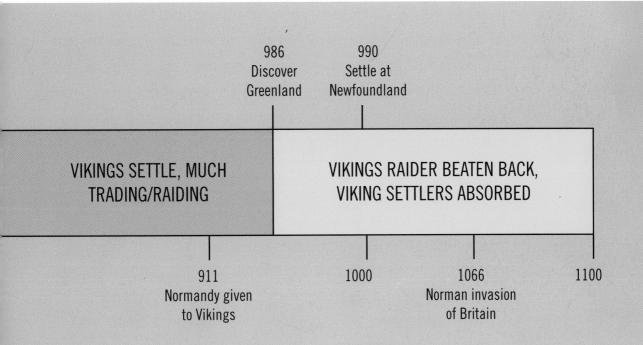

How were the Vikings ruled?

These chess pieces were made in about 1150. The third figure from the left shows a Viking king.

The Vikings did not have a single ruler. At first, they lived in villages made up of a few families. The leader of a village was the **jarl**. He did not make decisions on his own. He and all the other free men, or karls, of the village met regularly in a **Thing** to settle disputes, make laws, and punish crimes. Women, children, and **slaves** could not join in a Thing.

As time passed, the Vikings joined up into bigger groups to be safer from attack. Soon there were towns and large settlements with many jarls. Sometimes several groups agreed to work together, also for safety. Things became bigger and the jarls did not always agree. So the Viking lands split up into several kingdoms. Each was run by a king chosen by the jarls.

Viking society

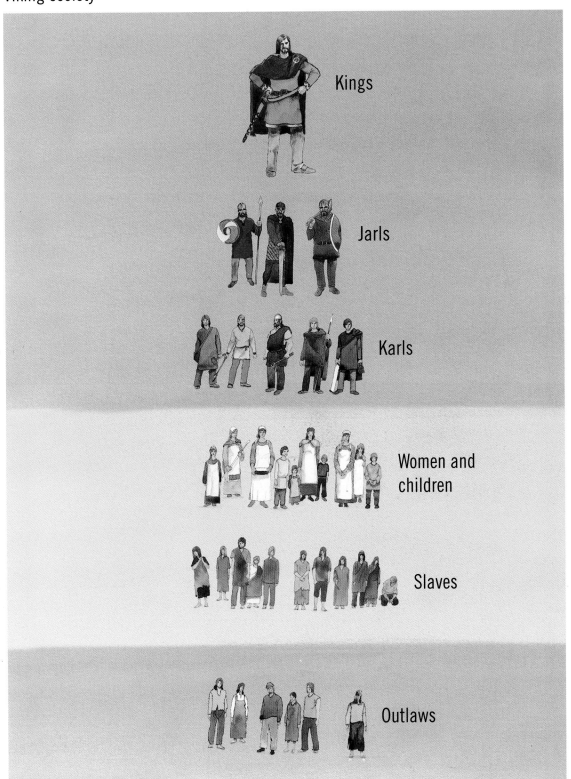

Kings

Jarls

Karls

Women and children

Slaves

Outlaws

War

War was part of the Viking way of life. Different villages or kingdoms would fight. Viking groups traded with each other when they could, but if they needed food or land that another group had, they were prepared to fight to take it. The Vikings also often had to fight when they arrived somewhere new. Every man over the age of 15 was supposed to have his own weapons and armour and be able to fight. The Vikings believed that a warrior who died in battle would go to a wonderful feasting hall in the afterlife called Valhalla.

These iron swords were found in the Viking city of Jorvik (now called York), in England. They are about 1,000 years old.

This stone was found on Lindisfarne, an island off the coast of England. It shows several warriors, usually said to be Vikings.

The Vikings fought with swords, axes, spears, and bows and arrows. They wore helmets and carried shields for protection. Some Vikings also wore chain mail. This was a **tunic** made from small links of metal joined together. Men from a village made their own fighting unit, which could have between 60 and 400 men. Because the groups were so small, they could recognize each other in battle. This was important, because many Viking groups had the same kind of armour and weapons. It could be hard to tell which side a person was on.

Religion

This tapestry shows three gods. Odin, the father of the gods and the god of wisdom, is carrying an axe. Thor, the god of war, is carrying a hammer. Frey, the god who made the crops grow, is carrying a stalk of corn.

At first, all Vikings were **pagans**. This means they believed in many different gods and goddesses that controlled different parts of everyday life. They told many stories about these gods and goddesses, who all lived together in big families – just like the Vikings. The gods and goddess argued, fought, and plotted against each other. They had to be kept happy, or they would stop the crops from growing, or make ships lose their way at sea. The Vikings also believed in other magical creatures such as trolls and **dwarfs**.

As they travelled, the Vikings met more and more Christians. They began to change their religion to Christianity. Sometimes they did this because Christians would only trade with other Christians. Some Vikings became Christians because they were forced to when they lost a war. Many Vikings just added Christianity to their old beliefs, even though Christians were supposed to stop believing in the Viking gods. When a Viking king became Christian, he made all his followers Christian, too.

The Viking goldsmith who owned this mould made crosses for Christians and tiny charms that were supposed to be Thor's hammer for pagans.

Ships

This ship from Oseburg, Norway, was made in about AD 850.
It was probably used for sailing on rivers or close to shore.

Ships were very important to the Vikings. They needed ships for exploring, **raiding**, trading, and carrying **settlers** to new lands. All Viking ships were built in the same way by overlapping planks of wood. They had to be narrow and shallow so they could sail up rivers. They all had square sails and a steering oar at the back. They were rowed with oars.

The smallest Viking ship, used by local traders, was 6.5 metres (21 feet) long and 1.4 metres (4.5 feet) wide. The largest to be discovered so far is 23.3 metres (76 feet) long and 5.2 metres (17 feet) wide.

The Vikings were among the first people to sail out of sight of land. They could do this by using the Sun or stars to **navigate**. If they could not see the sky, they used a lodestone to navigate. This was a stone that was magnetic, so it swung towards the north, like a **compass**.

The Vikings travelled long distances in their biggest boats. Everyone kept their belongings in chests. They sat on the chests to row. They slept on the deck and cooked food by lighting a fire in a box of sand.

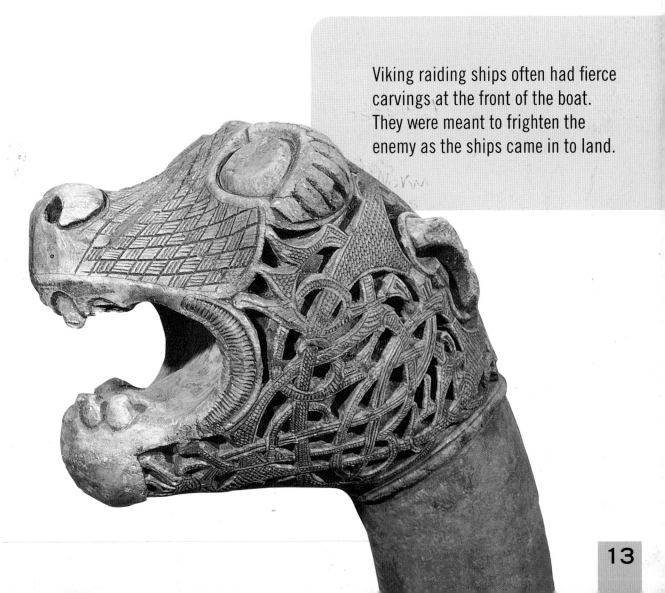

Viking raiding ships often had fierce carvings at the front of the boat. They were meant to frighten the enemy as the ships came in to land.

Expansion

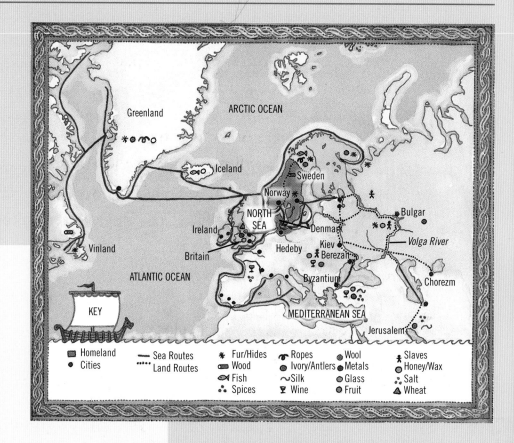

KEY

🖼 Homeland	— Sea Routes	✱ Fur/Hides	⚓ Ropes	◉ Wool	♀ Slaves
● Cities	⋯ Land Routes	▭ Wood	◉ Ivory/Antlers	◉ Metals	◉ Honey/Wax
		◀ Fish	∼ Silk	◉ Glass	∴ Salt
		∴ Spices	♈ Wine	◉ Fruit	△ Wheat

This map shows Viking trade routes and the places they settled.

Starting in AD **860**, the Vikings **raided** and **settled** in more and more places. They did this for several reasons. Travelling and raiding were part of the Viking way of life. Also, the further they travelled, the more places they found to trade with. An important reason for them to settle in other places was that their homelands did not have much good farming land. As the Viking population grew, there were too many people to feed or find homes for. They needed to find new places to live.

The Vikings travelled all over the world. You can see where they went on the map opposite. They were looking for people to trade with, or to take things from without trading, or both.

Travelling by sea could be hard in the winter, so if they found a place they liked, they would spend the winter there. Sometimes, they would settle there and bring their families to join them.

This Viking penny was found in Maine in 1957. Vikings probably did not live there, but other people living in Maine may have traded for it. The front and back of the penny are shown here.

Trade

Viking traders often carried their own scales and weights. The trader would put metal coins in one dish and a weight in the other. If they balanced, he knew it was a fair trade.

We know which countries the Vikings traded with because **goods** from other countries have been found in Viking graves, towns, and settlements. The Vikings sailed to most of the places that they traded with. They went by sea all around Spain and into the Mediterranean Sea. They sailed up rivers, too, especially wide European rivers like the Volga and the Dnieper.

Viking traders brought back silver from Russia, silks and spices from the Middle East, and wine from France. Coins from as far away as Arabia have been found in graves in the Orkney Islands, off Scotland.

The Vikings traded furs, fat, and **slaves** for the silks and spices they wanted. Viking towns such as Jorvik became trading centres for merchants from Germany, Ireland, and the Viking homelands.

Viking traders brought back goods from all over the world. This beautiful gold necklace was found in Sweden, but it probably came from far away.

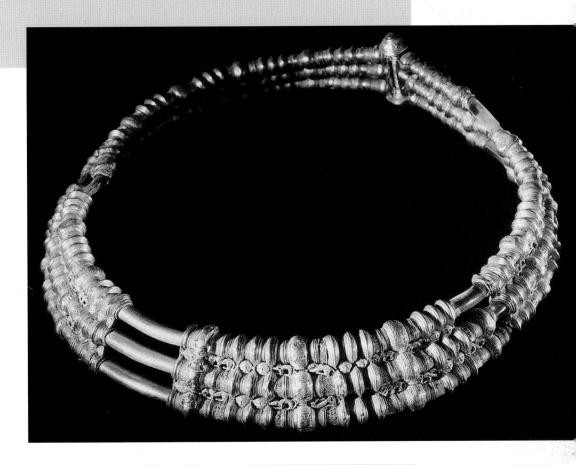

Towns

Most Vikings were farmers. They lived in small villages made up of large family groups. However, there were also many Viking craft workers and traders. These people needed to live and work in large settlements. Towns of different sizes sprang up in the places where the Vikings **settled**. Some of them were quite small. Others were larger – Jorvik had about 15,000 people living there at one time.

Viking towns were built on the coasts or on rivers wide enough for Viking ships to sail up. They had narrow streets. The houses and workshops were made from wood, with **thatched** roofs. Craft workers often lived in the same area, which made trading easier. People mainly traded from the street in front of their workshops. Animals were traded on market days at open spaces outside the town.

This modern artist's view shows how the town of Jorvik would have looked from the air when it was at its biggest. It developed into the modern city of York, England.

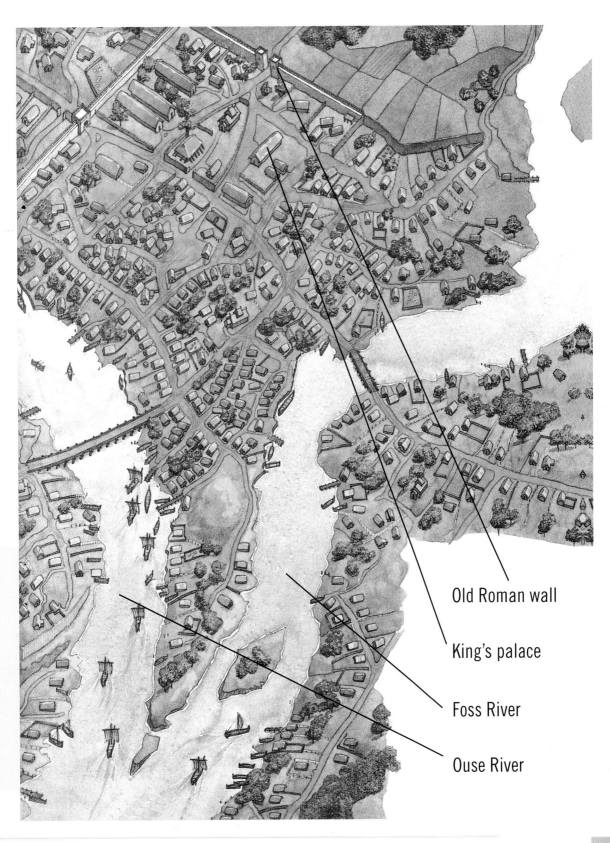

Old Roman wall

King's palace

Foss River

Ouse River

Houses

Wherever the Vikings settled, they built homes from the local materials. In Iceland, which had very little stone or wood, they built long, low houses. The walls and roofs were made from **turf**. In Shetland, there was enough stone to build the houses from stone. In Jorvik, houses were made from wood, with **thatched** roofs.

To iron clothes, Viking women used flat boards like this one, made from wood, bone, or stone. They ironed the clothes by smoothing them with a large, flat stone.

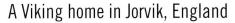

A Viking home in Jorvik, England

The beaten earth hearth had stone walls surrounding it for safety. The fire was used for heat and cooking.

Viking women wove their own cloth on looms like these.

The toilet was outside the house, but not too far away.

The wide benches down either side of the house were used for sleeping or sitting.

Some homes had coops like this, to shut chickens in at night to keep them safe.

Food and farming

Viking farmers grew different crops, depending on the weather where they lived. They all grew some kind of grain crop, such as wheat or barley, that could be used to make porridge, beer, and flour for bread. After the busy planting and **harvesting** time, farmers often went **raiding** to fill the gaps in their food supply.

Viking farmers kept chickens, geese, and ducks for eggs and meat. They kept cows, sheep, and goats for milk and meat, and pigs for meat. They used every part of the animals after they were killed. For example, skins were made into leather shoes or clothes, while bones were made into combs, pins, and blades for ice skates.

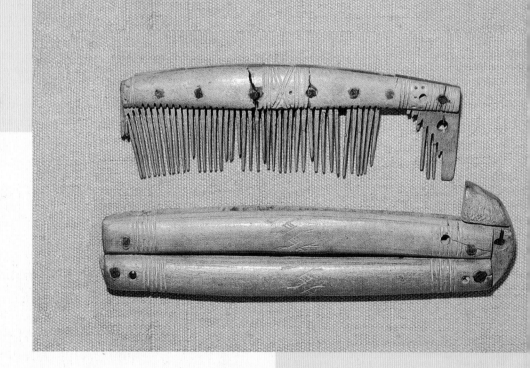

Vikings often made combs from the antlers of red deer. This comb has its own case.

The Vikings ate a lot of meat and fish, cooked over an open fire. They usually drank milk or beer. The two main meals of the day were eaten in the morning and in the early evening.

When people got married, or if there was a successful raid or some other reason for celebrating, they held a feast. The feast could last for several days. There would be speeches and storytelling, and whole animals would be **roasted** for eating. The men ate separately from the women and children. This kind of feast was for men only.

This model of a Viking hearth shows cooking pots found in Iceland.

Families

The Vikings lived in large family groups. There were more people in a family group than just the parents and children. This was partly because many of the men spent a lot of time away, **raiding**, trading, or exploring.

Families often passed the long wintertime by playing games. This board is for a battle game.

This scene is part of a tour of the re-created city of Jorvik. The man is using a foot-powered machine to make a wooden bowl.

Boys were taught a trade and how to fight. They learned the trade of the person who brought them up. Sometimes this was the same trade as their father, but not always. Girls were taught how to run a home and bring up children. They had to learn how to cook, sew, and weave.

Women learned to run their husband's farm or business, too, so they could keep things going when the men were away raiding or exploring. However, they were expected to obey their husbands. They did not help to make decisions.

Clothes

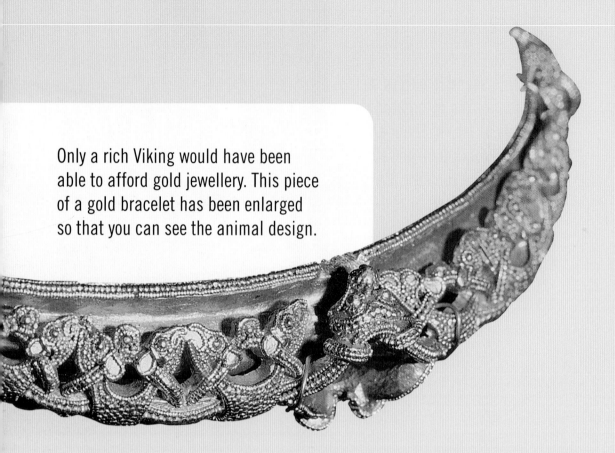

Only a rich Viking would have been able to afford gold jewellery. This piece of a gold bracelet has been enlarged so that you can see the animal design.

The Vikings wore warm, comfortable clothes. Most women spun, dyed, and wove the cloth for the family's clothes at home. Most cloth was spun from wool, although in some places **linen** was used. All cloth was dyed with dyes made from plants.

Slaves made the cloth and the clothes for rich families. Very rich people might buy silk cloth at markets. Shoes and boots were made of leather. Vikings who lived in cold places lined their boots and cloaks with sheepskin or fur.

Women often wore an apron over their dress, unless they were wealthy and not expected to do dirty work. Linen aprons were easier to wash and dry than heavy woollen dresses.

Children wore the same kind of clothes as adults.

Merchants who did a lot of trading often dressed well. They sometimes wore new kinds of clothes, brought back from their travels. This merchant is wearing baggy knee-length trousers, not the more typical long straight ones.

Kings and **jarls** wore the same kind of clothes as everyone else. But their clothes were made of more expensive materials, such as silk and fur.

Writing and storytelling

The Vikings had a system of writing that used alphabet symbols called **runes**. The earliest runic alphabet had 26 symbols, but by AD 700 there were only 16.

Runes were used in carvings on stone markers and gravestones. They were sometimes used to keep records of trading.

The Vikings loved **sagas** – stories that often mixed up real history and made-up adventures. Sagas almost always had a hero who faced great dangers and dealt with the gods, but won in the end. Because runes took so long to carve, they were not used to write down the sagas or other stories.

This memorial stone has runes carved all around the edge.

This carving from a Viking church is part of a series that tells the saga of Sigurd. The story is full of **dwarfs**, gold, revenge, and dragons. This scene shows a murder.

Instead, the Vikings had storytellers called *skalds* who told the sagas at feasts or on other special occasions. The sagas were very long, but they often rhymed. This made them easier to remember. A really good storyteller would change the sagas depending on the audience. If they were bored he would make the story shorter, or he would string out the parts they were really enjoying.

Some storytellers also made up poetry. Poems were shorter than sagas and did not always tell a story. They also made up riddles, which the Vikings loved.

End of the empire

This part of the Bayeux Tapestry shows the Norman invasion of Britain in 1066. The Norman ships look a lot like Viking ships. This is because Vikings had settled in Normandy.

The Vikings were not suddenly beaten in battle. Those who had moved to live in other places settled there. They often changed their ways and married into the local families. They became French or English or Russian. They no longer thought of themselves as Vikings. Those people who still lived in the Viking homelands **raided** less as Europe began to change and develop into more settled kingdoms. These kingdoms were not as easy to raid. So the Vikings settled for trading instead.

Glossary

compass   device with a magnetic needle that always points north

dwarf   in Viking stories, dwarfs were small human-like creatures

goods   things made or grown to trade or sell

harvest   season when crops are gathered; to gather a crop

hearth   area in front of a fireplace

jarl   Viking leader who ranked below the king

linen   smooth, strong cloth made from the flax plant

navigate   to find the right direction during a journey

pagan   person who believes in many gods and goddesses

raid   to attack a place, take what you want, and then leave

roast   to cook for a long time in an oven

rune   symbol in Viking writing

saga   Viking story containing history and fables

settler   someone who goes to a new land to live and work

slave   someone who belongs to someone else and is forced to work without pay

thatched   having a roof made out of grass or other plants

Thing   group of Vikings who met to make decisions

tunic   garment shaped like a knee-length T-shirt

turf   soil held together by the roots of grass and other plants

Find out more

Books to read
The History of Britain: The Saxons & Vikings, Brenda Williams
  (Heinemann Library, 2006)
Picture the Past: Life on a Viking Ship, Jane Shuter (Heinemann Library, 2005)

Using the Internet
Explore the Internet to find out more about the Vikings. Use a search engine, such as www.yahooligans.com or www.internet4kids.com and type in a keyword or phrase such as "Jorvik" or "runes".

Index